First Church of Christ,
Scientist, Berkeley

Phaidon Press Ltd
140 Kensington Church Street
London W8 4BN

First published 1994

© 1994 Phaidon Press Limited

ISBN 0 7148 2997 8

A CIP catalogue record for this
book is available from the British
Library.

Library of Congress Cataloguing
in Publication Data available.

Printed in Singapore

First Church of Christ, Scientist, Berkeley

Bernard Maybeck

Edward R Bosley

ARCHITECTURE IN DETAIL

Φ

Foreword
William Marquand
Emeryville, California

Called upon to build a church for a new sect [Maybeck] asked them about their beliefs, and was given testimony of such measureless confidence in their creed that he said it seemed a faith that had not been in the world since Christ was in the flesh. Then his problem, to him, was to design a church that would satisfy the joyous, holy feelings of an early Christian; perhaps an apostle. The result is a gilded, painted, grey and golden, blue and silver glory of Byzantine and Gothic elements that makes the heart sing to look at it.

Frank Morton Todd
Palace of Fine Arts and Lagoon
Paul Elder & Company
San Francisco, 1915

In common with other artists Virginia Woolf believed that the year 1910 brought a basic shift in human nature. Although we can see fundamental changes through generations of art, in retrospect we often remember only images of 'before' and 'after'. In works like First Church of Christ, Scientist, Berkeley, however, we see change at its vortex, a cohesive ensemble of ancient motifs and novel experimentation.

To Bernard Maybeck architecture is built art, and the ages of man's art manifest the whole of his being. While many architects of the new era would pursue a pared-down aesthetic of function, with the Christian Science church Maybeck provides a rare look inside the rich, expansive totality of man. Nested on a modest corner in Berkeley, its interior orchestrates aspects of our collective nature, offering such examples as the intimate sanctity of a Medieval chapel, the common-sense pragmatism of a modern factory, the thundering exuberance of Romantic opera, the rustic beauty of a fireside folk song. Virtually every ambience that Maybeck admired, including influences from Asia, takes part in this music, and does so with an honesty, unity, and beauty inspired, in part, by its patron.

In that sense the building was more than the work of a single creative talent. It was a collaboration with a congregation seeking a home. Edward Bosley's ground-breaking essay portrays the construction of the church as the unfolding of many unique aspirations and resources – it was the blossoming of an exotic flower.

Still, the church is thoroughly Maybeck and is widely regarded as his masterpiece. What was it, exactly, that would stir Maybeck's talents to full bloom?

Historically it is easy to classify Maybeck as a Romantic but this simply describes the wardrobe of what was an incredibly resilient self-styled artistic and spiritual identity. Uniquely, Maybeck proved impervious to the Age of Darwin marching alongside him, with its depiction of man as an aggressive bio-physical intellect. As brilliant as he could be, Maybeck felt that true creativity comes to a receptive heart, and is 'something no smart brain can figure out'. He often spoke of the marvellous inspiration he received as a youth in one of Paris's Medieval churches – to Maybeck, beauty is art's *summum bonum*, and it not only points to Beyond, it has its origins there.

To the Christian Scientists, this signified an essential truth. 'Spiritual sense', an idea with Puritan roots, was important to Mary Baker Eddy, the leader of the new movement. She taught that as we dwell on the things of God, Spirit, patterns of divine perfection begin to emerge in our own expression and experience.

The affinity that developed between the congregation and Maybeck was, however, more than spiritual. A prominent Episcopalian observed that Christian Science reawakened the world to the *workable* nature of Christianity. Members see it as the 'reinstatement of primitive Christianity and its lost element of healing'. Christian Scientists see Jesus' life as 'divinely natural', a healing life that was rooted in the here and now. One's spiritual life today, they insist, can have the same roots and the same useful, redeeming influence.

Maybeck marvelled at the sincerity of these claims. Like the angel in Wim Wenders's *Wings of Desire* Maybeck was 'spiritual', yet this son of a cabinet-maker, at home in the aroma of sawdust, yearned for an art 'rooted in the real, the practical, the utilitarian'. He took the commission with great anticipation and developed an abiding interest in this 'new-old' Scriptural teaching.

As for the Christian Scientists, their architecture was normally a customized Puritan meeting house, Byzantine dome, etc. In Berkeley, however, they sought a structure of the primal. They told Maybeck that foremost in his thought must be pure, divine qualities. The lives of early Christians shined with the beauty and power of God. These qualities, they reasoned, were just as available today.

This bond of hearts, minds, and aspirations proved special. The trust that the congregation placed in their architect became, in Maybeck's own heart, a simple confidence that God would work through his work. The results made him proud. His church hints, unlike any other building I am aware of, at the coherent whole of what we are.

6

1 (previous page) Bernard Maybeck, First Church of Christ, Scientist, Berkeley, 1910, auditorium.
2 Maybeck felling a tree in the mountains c1923.
3 Maybeck, seated at left, with friends and family at the Maybecks' log cabin in Ukiah, California, c1924.
4 San Francisco Swedenborgian Church, designed by A C Schweinfurth in the office of A Page Brown, 1894. Maybeck was a draughtsman in Brown's office at the time and assisted Schweinfurth with the design.

3

A touchstone of romanticized architecture, First Church of Christ, Scientist in Berkeley, California has stood, since 1910, as a paradigm of enigmatic beauty. Its eclectic and inventive design derives from Byzantine, Romanesque and Gothic traditions, but the date of construction and straightforward use of materials cast the church within the bounds of the American Arts and Crafts idiom. Its layered, complex exterior and bold structural system shun ecclesiastical norms, yet both are indispensable to the dynamism and intimacy of the dramatic auditorium, a space of worship which is so completely reassuring and right. It challenges attempts at categorization, but the ensemble of forms and forces at work has been so thoughtfully directed, skilfully proportioned, and beautifully detailed in the hands of the architect, Bernard Maybeck, that we revere the church today as a courageous and sublime building achievement.

Roots among old-world artisans

The legacy of Bernard Maybeck occupies an obscure niche in the history of American architecture, one which reflects his artistic, imaginative and idiosyncratic personality. Bernard Ralph Maybeck (1862–1957) was born into a family which hoped to raise him for artistic pursuits. His father, Bernhardt Maybeck, emigrated from his native Germany with his brother, Henry, to take advantage of the comparatively greater political and intellectual freedom of America after revolutionary upheavals swept Europe in 1848.[1] The two brothers apprenticed to

a Staten Island cabinet-maker, learning traditional European wood carving. Bernhardt met and married a fellow expatriate, Elisa Kern, and the two settled in Manhattan's Greenwich Village. Not far from their home, Bernhardt opened a cabinet shop specializing in bench-made furniture. Here, he exploited his carving talent while his partner, Joseph Reinal, executed joinery for their commissions. Work progressed well, and at home the birth of the Maybecks' son Bernard completed a happy domestic picture. Elisa died in 1865 when Ben (as Bernard came to be called) was only three. Despite Ben's youth, his mother had left him with a clear memory of her urging him to become an artist. His father was similarly inclined, encouraging his son to spend his evenings drawing.[2] Now a widower, Bernhardt left the cabinet-making partnership to join Pottier and Stymus, a large architectural carving and custom furniture firm, where he became foreman of carving.

As young Ben grew from childhood into adolescence he made satisfactory progress at school, but later at the College of the City of New York he ran into difficulties when confronted with the repetitive aspects of chemistry coursework. Probably sensing that his true calling would be outside the sciences, Maybeck left school to join his father at Pottier and Stymus where he apprenticed by running errands and tracing the occasional shop drawing of Pullman Parlor Cars, a major client.[3] Ben adjusted haltingly to the hierarchy and pressure of a commercial enterprise but developed confidence in his nascent drawing ability while designing an ingenious reversible Pullman seat. Believing that his real talent might lie in design, Bernhardt arranged for Ben to sail from New York in 1881 to take a position in the firm's Paris studio.

The Paris office of Pottier and Stymus was located in the Latin Quarter, not far from the Ecole des Beaux-Arts, the most respected academic institution of the day to train professional architects. Maybeck soon became attracted by the stylish appearance of the architecture students he saw in the boulevards. Recalling the elegant figure of an architect he had once seen in 'kid gloves and a pot hat', he believed that this profession would be his true destiny. With perhaps little notion of what the study of architecture at the prestigious Ecole des Beaux-Arts actually entailed, he sat the rigorous entrance examination and qualified, coming 22nd among the 250 applicants.[4]

A Classicist's training, a Medievalist's wanderings

At the Ecole, Maybeck was indoctrinated in the prevailing architectural tradition whose curriculum focused on a building's composition and character, stressing the grandeur of historical styles. The traditional emphasis at the Ecole had formerly disallowed the tenets espoused by John Ruskin and Eugène Emmanuel Viollet-le-Duc which championed the inherent value of craftsmanship and the natural expression of materials and functional expression of structure. Instead of the temples of ancient Greece and Rome, Ruskin and Viollet cited as their paradigm the Gothic cathedrals and their artisan-builders. Indeed, Viollet-le-Duc had taught non-Classicist ideals at the Ecole and was dismissed for this reason in 1867. By the time Maybeck had arrived, however, Viollet's concepts had been somewhat rehabilitated, enough to generate in Maybeck at least a long-lasting reverence for Medieval architecture. He recalled being taught that the plan of a building should generate its overall organization and aspect, and that the character of its elevations should reflect its intended use. Specifically, he was told that ' ... anyone can make elevations, but the plan is the backbone of anything beautiful'. This was more progressive than the Classicist line of thinking, and it was a useful concept, especially since Maybeck believed that 'beauty is the essence of architecture'.[5]

Maybeck received a sound training at the Ecole, but he wisely tempered it with his own investigations. He travelled to the cathedrals of the region, sketching and seeking inspiration at first hand. To his credit, he left Europe having sought as much from extra-curricular visits to Gothic and Romanesque churches as he had gained in the ateliers and classrooms of his formal instruction.

4

5 Charles Keeler in Grecian robes, dramatizing the myth of Berkeley as the 'Athens of the Pacific'.

6 Bernard Maybeck, Highland Place and Ridge Road houses designed between 1895 and 1899 in Berkeley's north side hills. Charles Keeler's house is second from the left.

7 Bernard Maybeck, George H Boke house, Berkeley, 1902. The Boke house shows Maybeck's ability simultaneously to expose numerous decorative and structural elements in wood.

5

Professional beginnings and influences

Returning to New York in 1886, Maybeck found work with Thomas Hastings, a friend from the Ecole, who, with John Carrère (another Ecole student), had recently left the renowned firm of McKim Mead and White to form their own, Carrère and Hastings. Their first commission was for a large resort hotel, the Ponce de Leon in St Augustine, Florida. Construction was already in progress when Maybeck joined the firm, but working on the Ponce de Leon and its sister hotel, the Alcazar, gave him a chance to test both his formal and informal European education.[6]

After leaving the east for a brief period of work in Kansas City (where he met his future wife, Annie White), Maybeck travelled to California in 1890. This move was prompted by encouraging reports of work to be had coming from Willis Polk, another young architect who had moved to San Francisco from New York and whose family Maybeck had also become acquainted with in Kansas City. Maybeck may also have chosen San Francisco to be closer to his cousin, the son of his father's brother, Henry.[7] Taking on a brief assignment with the firm of Wright and Sanders, Maybeck spent part of 1890 in Salt Lake City and returned to Kansas City in October to marry Annie White. The two moved west together late that year to set up their household in Oakland, near the eastern shore of San Francisco Bay.

An excellent draughtsman, Maybeck soon found employment, though not in an architect's office but with the Charles M Plum Company, interior designers and makers of custom furniture. Maybeck had been promised work, however, by the architect A Page Brown (1859–96), who had also recently come from New York. Brown operated a successful firm which included Willis Polk (1867–1924) and A C Schweinfurth (1864–1900), both of whom had worked for him in New York, coincidentally in the same building occupied by Maybeck's former employer Carrère and Hastings. The promised job with A Page Brown did not materialize until two years later, causing Maybeck to remain with the Plum Company longer than he might have preferred. Once in Brown's office, however, he was back in his element. He assisted A C Schweinfurth, Brown's chief designer, with the competition for the California Building at the World's Columbian Exposition in Chicago, and the Brown plan, including detailing by Maybeck, was ultimately chosen to represent the state at the fair in 1893. Its romantic references to the Franciscan missions of early California reflected a prevailing stylistic choice among California architects, but the dome, part of Maybeck's contribution, was heralded as innovative and promising. Maybeck was appointed construction supervisor in Chicago, a position that afforded him ample opportunity to scrutinize the highly-popular Exposition first-hand. The vast scale and romantic pomp of the main buildings, dubbed the 'White City', appealed to his Beaux-Arts roots, but Maybeck's active imagination and intellect retained an equal reverence for the romantic and anonymous Gothic builders, the craftsmen whose legacy was to play a key role in his future.

Following the Chicago Exposition, a formative collaboration for Maybeck was undoubtedly the commission which Brown had received to design the San Francisco Swedenborgian Church in 1894. While the extent of Maybeck's involvement in the rustic Swedenborgian project is undocumented, he is likely to have contributed to it, probably in decorative detailing, since A C Schweinfurth had primary design responsibility in Brown's office.[8] Through mutual friends, Maybeck knew the Swedenborgian Church client, the Reverend Joseph Worcester (himself an amateur architect), and admired the unpainted, wood-shingled home the minister had created for himself in 1876, long before the style became widely accepted.[9] Worcester's well-reasoned design concept for the church would have appealed strongly to Maybeck since it required taking unusual steps to reflect the natural surroundings, both in structure and materials. The most visible manifestation of Worcester's philosophy of building was the remarkable truss and knee-brace system which employed California madrone trees, exposed and with the bark left on. The resulting structure, and the nature-based design philosophy espoused by its influential pastor, were to become cornerstones of the Arts and Crafts movement in California.[10]

An individualist emerges in the 'Athens of the Pacific'

Despite his early experience designing public buildings, and a reputation which now rests on non-residential architecture (First Church of Christ, Scientist and the 1915 Palace of Fine Arts), Maybeck's early practice involved a significant amount of domestic architecture. After 1908, he designed several homes for wealthy clients in San Francisco, but his signature innovations were more persuasively developed in the earlier homes he had designed for upper-middle-class clients in the hills of the university town of Berkeley, across the bay. Berkeley's intelligentsia provided a congenial and fertile field for innovative architecture. Berkeley also offered the attraction of a somewhat sunnier climate than San Francisco, as well as spectacular topography near the shore of San Francisco Bay. Situated on a natural slope descending west, facing the dramatic isthmus of the Golden Gate, Berkeley was a quiet suburb of 13,000 at the turn of the twentieth century. It was a pastoral place well-suited to raising families in a setting close to nature, higher education and commerce. Maybeck's design and drafting

6

7

8 Mary Baker Eddy, Founder of The First Church of Christ, Scientist.

9 The First Church of Christ, Scientist: The Mother Church in Boston, Massachusetts, 1894. The larger Renaissance revival extension was completed in 1904.

8

talents, combined with his own romantic vision for the community's hillside neighbourhoods, were suited to the spirit of what became known as the 'Athens of the Pacific'.[11]

An important aesthetic collaboration and long-lasting friendship developed in 1891 between Maybeck and a young Berkeley poet, Charles Keeler. They met by chance, but partly because Keeler and Maybeck both stood out in their dress and demeanour. Keeler described sighting Maybeck in his Bohemian garb on the San Francisco ferry and compared it with his own affected style: 'Instead of a vest he wore a sash, and his suit seemed like homespun of a dark brown color ... Perhaps we were both sufficiently unusual in appearance to attract one another. In those days I used to wear an old-fashioned broadcloth cape ... [and] carried [a] gold-headed cane'.[12] The two men became friends. A sensitive and creative individual, Keeler was drawn to Maybeck's artistic opinions and became his first residential client in 1895. Both were later to become the primary proponents of Berkeley's artistic and rustic life-style.

A group of concerned and design-minded citizens was organized in 1898 as the Hillside Club. Its goal was to promote the ideals of a simple home life characterized by unpainted, shingle-clad houses surrounded by regionally-appropriate and sensitively-designed landscaping. Maybeck and Keeler figured prominently in this cause. During the first decade of the new century, when Berkeley's population more than trebled to 40,000, Hillside Club members reasoned that it was crucial in maintaining Berkeley's character that they promote the awareness of good design tenets during the inevitable building boom which would accompany rapid growth. Keeler's important 1904 essay, *The Simple Home*, gave voice to Maybeck's philosophies of design and became a virtual code, graciously imposed on the property owners and home builders of the Berkeley hills. It became the manifesto of the club – an appealing treatise on proper Berkeley hill life. In it, Keeler held forth on the virtues of simplicity, and illustrated his prose with photographs of Maybeck's houses, among others. Keeler wrote: 'In the Simple Home all is quiet in effect, restrained in tone, yet natural and joyous in its frank use of unadorned material. Harmony of line and balance of proportion is not obscured by meaningless ornamentation; harmony of color is not marred by violent contrasts. Much of the construction shows, and therefore good workmanship is required and the craft of the carpenter is restored to its old-time dignity'.[13] These words could have been (and probably were, at one time or another) intoned by Maybeck himself.

Maybeck's domestic architectural practice began to take root and flourish. Notoriety came not only from his distinctive manner of home-building – inventive floor plans, interiors of unpainted redwood, exteriors of unpretentious wood shingles – but also from his high-profile connection with the driving force in Berkeley, the University of California. Phoebe Apperson Hearst, philanthropic widow of mining millionaire Senator George Hearst, had acted on a suggestion from Maybeck to sponsor an international competition to design a master plan for the university. In 1896, at the age of 34, Maybeck was put in charge of administering the competition and establishing guidelines. He travelled with Annie throughout Europe to consult with jurors, and with Mrs Hearst attended the judging of the first round of submissions. Maybeck's important role in the competition, while it brought the criticism inevitable to such projects, also helped him gain invaluable experience as well as a reputation for having a strong architectural vision. The competition absorbed Maybeck's attention for several years and kept his name and achievements in the public eye. During the decade following the conclusion of the university competition, Maybeck grew to the height of his creative powers, undertaking nearly a hundred design projects of one kind or another over the ten-year period. It was during this busy period of his career, at the age of 47, that Maybeck was presented with the opportunity to design his masterpiece, First Church of Christ, Scientist, Berkeley.

A young and pioneering church

The Christian Science faith was relatively new, having been formally founded in New England by Mary Baker Eddy in 1879. Loosely associated with late-nineteenth-century alternative religious movements, the church enjoyed steady growth despite its unorthodox teachings, especially those regarding healing outside the mainstream medical profession. Christian Science churches held primarily to prevailing architectural forms, especially Classic and Renaissance revivals which had been popularized at the Chicago Exposition in 1893. Perhaps because its teachings were unfamiliar and often criticized by the uninitiated, most branch churches may have sought to minimize the attention paid to them through largely non-controversial and even unremarkable architecture. Mrs Eddy's teachings on the building of new structures emphasizes spirituality and calls for little fanfare: 'No large gathering of people nor display shall be allowed when laying the Corner Stone of a Church of Christ, Scientist. Let the ceremony be devout. No special trowel should be used'.[14] Mrs Eddy did not elaborate on what an ideal church edifice should look like. The First Church of Christ, Scientist in Boston, Massachusetts, known as The Mother Church, combined its original Richardson-inspired structure (1893–4) with an imposing extension of Renaissance revival design completed in 1904. When a branch church desired to erect a new building, there were few stylistic guidelines beyond the diversity of existing Christian Science structures.

Berkeley members organize and purchase land

In Berkeley, the Christian Science Church was formed officially in 1905 as an offshoot of a larger church in neighbouring Oakland. Informal meetings had taken place in homes and meeting halls since 1897. Immediately after the official organization of the Berkeley church the Board of Directors (now Executive Board) appointed a 'committee on the selection of a lot for building'.[15] Several parcels were considered, including a building site at the intersection of Dwight Way and Bowditch Street. An option was also proposed to 'buy the Congregational Church and move it to another lot ... offered for $7,000'. This idea was apparently of scant interest, since the next entry in the minutes returns to the subject of the corner lot at Dwight and Bowditch. The actual purchase of the property proceeded rather unsteadily at first. The original offering price was recorded in the minutes of 31 March 1905 as $7,500 for the 100 x 150ft lot, or $6,000 for a smaller 100 x 100ft sub-division on the same parcel of land. In May, the committee reported that their offer of $7,250 for the entire lot had been declined, and that the asking price of $7,500 had been re-confirmed. By the June 1st meeting, however, the asking price for the large lot had risen to $8,000. No discussion regarding the price discrepancy was recorded in the minutes, but in an effort to secure the figure from further fluctuation, and in an impressive show of support for the whole endeavour, the assembled directors personally pledged sufficient gifts and loans to secure the purchase of the land.[16]

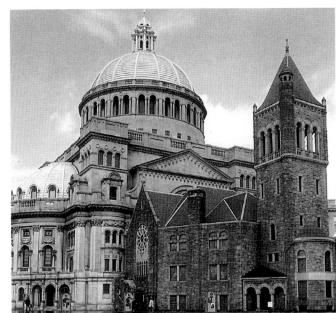

9

12 **10** Julia Morgan, St John's Presbyterian Church, Berkeley, 1908–10. While the exterior has a dignified, if domestic, scale, the interior recalls a vernacular barn with its simple, exposed trusses.

Over the next few years, as church membership grew, funds were raised for a building. On 22 October 1908, a meeting of the board of directors convened to appoint a committee to investigate and propose a new church building. At a full membership meeting in November, a vote was even taken on the building material they would prefer: 21 voted in favour of wood, 50 for stone. A minimum budget of $25,000 was set, with no upward limit.

10

The search for an architect
In August of 1909, the newly-formed Plans Committee made up of five women, met to consider hiring an architect, a charge given to them by the 25-member Building Committee. Notes recorded later by Plans Committee chairwoman, Eulora Jennings, state: 'it was the opinion of all of the members ... that it would be desirable to have some plans by prominent architects ...'.[17] She reported that among others, the Plans Committee visited St John's Church, a dramatic wooden hall designed for the Presbyterian Church by Julia Morgan in 1908. Morgan was a gifted protégée of Maybeck's, and with his help in the late-1890s became the first woman ever admitted to the Ecole des Beaux-Arts.[18] Eulora Jennings noted that St John's Church 'cost about $6,000 and seats five hundred'. As they visited the church, the committee would have had to visualize what Morgan might do with a budget more than four times greater. The notes make no mention of Morgan (or Maybeck) by name, but state that the same day, after the St John's visit, a 'committee of three' went to San Francisco to 'interview the architects'. One had apparently moved and could not be found. Jennings writes: 'The others both said substantially the same thing, that it was not customary with them to submit plans – that this was very

unsatisfactory both to them and would be so to us, and that the thing for us to do was to settle upon one architect and then have him work out what we wanted'.[19] It is a matter of speculation that Maybeck himself might have been the one who provided this bit of advice, but the committee was ultimately persuaded to accept it.

No judgements, good or bad, were recorded regarding any of the buildings or architects the Plans Committee visited that day. According to his own account, Maybeck initially declined the invitation to design the church, but during a second visit from the committee – this time with all five members in attendance – he became convinced (and possibly flattered), that the women were serious and sincere in their desire to hire him. At the first meeting he recalled telling the committee that: 'it couldn't be done', probably referring to the committee's clear notion of what they wanted and Maybeck's doubt that their vision might coincide with his. At the second meeting he softened, recalling that 'they consulted God before they came to see their architect – they told me so ... And then I made up my mind that since they were so very sincere about it there must be something to it. And since that time, I believe that God had all to do with it'.[20]

One gets the impression from the accumulated evidence, especially a noticeable lack of broad debate over the selection of an architect, that the committee may have been adopted by Maybeck nearly as much as he was by them. His gentle and thoughtful personality and even his artistic manner of dress must have made a persuasive impression on the committee. They were familiar with his work living among his ubiquitous shingled designs in the Berkeley hills and at least one member of the larger Building

Committee, John Gilson Howell, had close contact with Maybeck's work.[21] Before opening his own antiquarian bookshop in 1912, Howell worked for Paul Elder in the San Francisco shop which bore his name. In 1906, Maybeck designed a temporary replacement for the shop, which had been destroyed in the city's disastrous earthquake and fire, and in 1908 designed its permanent interior in an existing building. It is worth noting that Maybeck's decorative use of Gothic tracery in the Paul Elder Shop is nearly identical to much of what he designed later in First Church of Christ, Scientist. Paul Elder's parents, Scott and Mary Elder, were also both active in the church. Mary became a member of the Building Committee in March 1911 when construction was under way.[22]

The Plans Committee's final report on the search for an architect was made to the larger Building Committee on 27 September 1909, concluding: '[The] committee has considered some five or six sets of plans that have been submitted and have also considered some twelve or thirteen architects. We have made visits to several of these. We unanimously report that in our opinion Mr Maybeck would understand best what our wants are and is best qualified to express them in this building. It is from our talks with him that many of the ideas expressed in the foregoing recommendations have originated. We are not to present any plans to him, but give him simply this statement of our needs & allow him to work out the building with this as a basis'.[23] The trust

inherent in this statement is revealing. The committee, headed by an artist, Eulora Jennings, was deeply respectful of the need to allow another artist's vision to evolve, without holding it blindly to strict dictates. This may have grated on a membership which had gone so far as to vote on the material to be used in construction. The closing sentences of the Plans Committee report hint of tension and even defensiveness about the selection process, unintentionally confirming that Maybeck may have been the only one the committee had seriously considered: 'We shall be glad to inform any of the committee as to what architects we have considered. It is hardly necessary to bespeak your cordial and loyal support of the one that has been chosen'. Some members of the Building Committee had obviously disapproved of the eccentric Maybeck or felt that the Plans Committee had acted hastily in selecting an architect.[24] But when it came to a vote, the committee's recommendation to retain Mr Maybeck was adopted by the 25-member Building Committee.

11

12

13

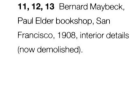

11, 12, 13 Bernard Maybeck, Paul Elder bookshop, San Francisco, 1908, interior details (now demolished).

13

14 First Church of Christ
Scientist, Berkeley. Maybeck's
presentation rendering of interior
looking northeast. A number
of details shown here were
included in the finished
auditorium.

15 Following the original
landscape plan, wisteria partially
obscures the west tracery
window of the church, bringing
nature closer to the interior.

An early Christian vision for the church
When asked to remember how he
conceived the design of the church,
Maybeck recalled late in his life that his
sense of the committee's sincerity
reminded him of the early Christians. This
would have been appreciated by his clients
as a positive sign, since their founder, Mrs
Eddy, had sought to 'establish a church ...
which should reinstate primitive Christianity
and its lost element of healing'. An
endearing quirk was Maybeck's tendency
to categorize his clients according to the
historical era he believed befitted them.
He implied that he had assigned the
Medieval Romanesque period to the
devout committee of Christian Scientists,
possibly because of their founder's well-
known quest to rehabilitate ancient aspects
of Christian faith.[25] In particular, Maybeck
related that he began the design process
for the church by contemplating what a
twelfth-century builder would do with such
a commission. In a partial flight of
hyperbole, he described the final product
as '... pure Romanesque made out of
modern materials', confirming that his
intention had been to develop the
Medieval theme.[26]

The design programme
The programme to guide the design of the
church was recorded in a 14-page
handwritten recommendation, a thoughtful
and thorough instruction covering all
aspects of the church edifice from the
character of the building to the provision
of space for the heating and ventilation
equipment. It opens with the charge that:
'The Church should be a perfect concept
of mental architectural skill, manifesting
unity, harmony, beauty, light and peace.
A structure denoting progress in all lines
and strictly individual in character, designed
to meet our present needs and in keeping
with the artistic surroundings. It should
express simplicity and beauty'. A quote
from Mary Baker Eddy was also included
in the document and may have struck
a sympathetic chord with Maybeck:
'Mrs Eddy says ... "Beauty is a thing of life
which dwells forever in the eternal Mind
and reflects the charms of His goodness
in expression, form, outline, and color"'. In
closing, the programme credits Maybeck's
help in developing the goals in consultation
with the committee, further suggesting that
he was a clear, and perhaps early, favourite
in the selection process.[27]

14

A design of few compromises

The first official conceptualization of the church on paper was a series of coloured sketches which Maybeck presented with his interpretation to the Building Committee at a meeting on 17 January 1910. The Plans Committee warned the larger committee in their written report: 'Mr Maybeck ... expressed a wish to have the Building Committee fully apprised of the scheme for a building which he had in mind, stating that it was somewhat unusual and he did not wish to have any surprises confront the committee later on'. The coloured sketches depict a church so similar to what was actually built, that they stand as persuasive evidence that Maybeck was in firm control of his clients' hearts and minds from the beginning of the design process. Among the surviving preliminary coloured renderings by Maybeck, the primary axis-of-entry side, the south elevation, shows an east–west pergola and trellis structure interrupted by an entry gate of Gothic tracery design, separating the portico from the street.[28] Above and behind the main portico looms the high, shadowy form of the main roof, its gable hidden by deeply projecting eaves. Left of the portico, a pergola structure is supported by fluted concrete columns topped with decorated capitals in a geometric theme. The pergola's columns, as well as the trellis columns east of the portico, is depicted almost to resemble the remains of an ancient temple. They seem separate from the main building and give the appearance of a romantic ruin, complete with encroaching vegetation. Behind the columns, the core building appears, looking more complete and intact, as if it had been built centuries later.

A second exterior sketch, a pastel, is a perspective taken from the west elevation looking north along Bowditch Street. Wisteria vines are shown as mature plantings, entwined amid the concrete pillars. A third sketch shows the rich interior detail Maybeck envisioned, much of which remarkably survived committee reviews and inevitable budget adjustments. But perhaps the greatest tribute to Maybeck's power of architectural vision is how accurately the rendering communicates the Medieval mood of the main auditorium space as it was built. Maybeck's signature Gothic tracery panels in the sketch are remarkably similar to those finally installed, and the colours chosen to enliven the concrete piers in the preliminary drawing are of the same palette as those ultimately used.

15

18

19

16 West elevation taken from the southwest corner of Dwight Way and Bowditch Street, c1911.

17 West elevation, c1913. Photo taken from northwest, opposite property line on Bowditch Street. Note the 'well-head' design of ventilation outlet surmounted by a planter box and pitched roof.

18 East window. Maybeck's interpretation of Gothic tracery is carried out in concrete on pre-fabricated steel armatures. Here and throughout the church decorative complexity increases from bottom to top.

19 Music cabinet, designed by Maybeck, is flanked by industrial sash in west end of narthex.

16

17

Construction and occupancy

Maybeck's sketches were approved at the next meeting of the Building Committee and exhibited for the review of church members. For this purpose, a room in a local bank building was rented and staffed for one week by committee members who were appointed to explain the drawings. This phase of scrutiny passed with no objections being brought at the full membership meeting on the 5th of February, and on the 28th Maybeck was asked to 'proceed with greatest possible rapidity to complete the details of the plans'.[29] These were completed in Maybeck's office, and included small changes and additions voted for by the committee. In June, Charles F Wieland, church member and chair of the Construction Committee, was formally engaged as Supervisor of Construction to act in the capacity of general contractor. Low bidder William L Boldt was chosen as primary building contractor in August and a building permit was issued on 26 September 1910, nearly one year to the day after the Building Committee had approved the selection of Bernard Maybeck as architect.

The construction and furnishing of the church was an elaborate committee endeavour for the church membership. Sub-committees had been established from the 25 members of the Building Committee to oversee separately general construction, landscaping and grounds, furnishings, the pipe organ and finances. Despite the seeming obstacle of involving so many committees and individuals, a relative working harmony and rhythm seems to have been achieved. The building was ready to occupy for services on Wednesday evening, 16 August 1911, less than a year after construction had begun.[30]

Exterior forms of truth and beauty

The finished product of First Church of Christ, Scientist, Berkeley surpassed the expectations of its delighted members. In an interview some years later, one member remarked: 'We wanted a church by Mr Maybeck ... but we never dreamed of such a beautiful thing'.[31] Maybeck had promised a 'somewhat unusual' structure, but also said he would pursue a truthful use of materials. Both sentiments reflected his natural inclination to search for beauty in his designs.[32]

Seen from the street, the exterior forms seem kinetic. The eye is drawn briskly from one form to the next, from the stepped and separated masses of the concrete planting boxes at the foundation level to the hyperactive interplay of surface planes and roof-lines, and the intricately articulated pergola and trellis structures. But visually colliding elements of the composition also alternate with more serene, comforting signals of vernacular domestic architecture – the low angle of the roofs, heavy wood posts, exposed beam ends and rafters – all an elaboration of the Craftsman idiom. The only overt ecclesiastical references are the exquisite Gothic tracery windows which punctuate three elevations. Despite a profusion of elements which might have conflicted, with potentially unfortunate results in less sensitive hands, Maybeck managed to finesse it all, blending diversity with grace and dignity to earn an awed respect.

Materials used on the exterior range from the mundane to the curious. Simple concrete, reinforced and poured into

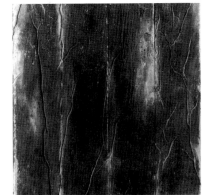

20

21

board forms, predominates on the ground level. Industrial sash windows, not unprecedented but certainly atypical in a church project, were supplied under modest protest from the fabricator. In refusing to reply to the architect's initial request for a bid, the Detroit Steel Products Company elicited this frustrated response from Maybeck's office: '... you say you do not recommend [industrial steel sash] for use in churches. You of course do not understand the nature of the work in which we wish to use them ... and will again ask you to kindly quote us on [them] ...'.[33] The sash was ultimately produced by the reluctant supplier. It was then installed and glazed with 'antique clear glass'. During the glazing process, the panes were bisected by vertical leading to give a lighter, more delicate appearance to the windows.

An asbestos insulation material, 'asbestos lumber', was specified for exterior walls in areas not filled with steel sash or board and batten panelling. These inexpensive asbestos panels were also highly improbable for use on a church exterior, but they nonetheless approximate the colour of the concrete used on the ground level, promoting a thorough visual unity. The panels are enlivened by Maybeck's clever use of small red squares of the same material, which, when rotated 45 degrees, became decorative diamonds which helped to secure the larger panels where they join.

Maybeck specified planter boxes on the roof above the steel sash windows of the west elevation. Planters also topped the elaborate exterior ventilation ducts, structures which look convincingly like well-heads but are actually the extension of interior piers. Maybeck used overhead planters on other projects, including the

22

23

17

20 Square sheets of 'asbestos lumber' serve as exterior cladding, and are held in place by smaller red squares of the same material.
21 Interior concrete wall with rivulets caused by wrinkling of the paper lining the board forms.
22 Partial view of east elevation, taken from garden court between main church and Sunday School addition. Original standing seam sheet-metal roof later covered by tile roof.
23 Vine-laden trellis structures surmount each concrete column along the south elevation. Exposed beams supported by the capitals are extensions of the truss system on the interior of the Fireplace room.
24 West elevation, showing the planned integration of plantings and structure. The deep eaves are supported by carved beam ends which project through from the interior.

24

25

26

27

18

25 Detail of stone capital at Cluny, from Maybeck's sketchbook of French Romanesque churches, undated.

26 Capital at St Trophine, Arles.

27 Column detail in cathedral at Beaune, showing square-fluted shaft.

28 Detail of figure attached to column, from unidentified church.

29 South elevation columns with intricate build-up of trellis structure. Column shafts and figures show the influence of French Romanesque details recorded in Maybeck's sketchbook.

30 Cornerstone of the church with decorative features from early Christian architecture.

Leon L Roos house (1909) and the immense Palace of Fine Arts exhibition hall and rotunda for San Francisco's Panama-Pacific Exposition of 1915. The high planters at the palace were never used as intended, but the idea was to create the instant impression of a grand, Classical ruin. Similarly, at the church, the high planters were part of the landscaping plan to create the effect of an aged structure, and to mitigate the starkness of the concrete and factory-sash windows.

The planters were later removed, probably because they leaked or were difficult for a gardener to maintain. By the time they were deleted, however, the desired effect of overflowing greenery and blooms was already assured by wisteria which had climbed the height of four massive, 14 x 14in posts which flank the west tracery window. The posts are tied back to the transept by pairs of profiled rafters, the whole structure being surmounted by a delicate, multi-layered trellis. A smaller trellis carries the same vine the length of the eaves, assuring an abundant riot of colour in the spring.

On the south elevation, as shown in the presentation drawings, the elaborate columns of the trellis east of the portico are the visually-dominant element, positioned rhythmically between the expanses of steel sash. The square flutes of the columns are reminiscent of those in a detail sketch Maybeck made from the Burgundian cathedral of Beaune years before. The cast concrete capitals also derive, in spirit at least, from French Romanesque antecedents, possibly Ste Madeleine at Vézelay. But whatever their origin, the stooped, veiled figures, as if on pilgrimage to a healing, establish a convincing early Christian theme to reflect the underlying roots of Christian Science.

29

30

28

31

The entry: a calming transition

Covered walks along both entry axes offer areas of quiet approach to the interior of the church. Both major and minor points of access are open and direct, fulfilling the programme stipulation that the church should 'express welcome to all, exemplified in its entrance'. The longer, secondary approach from the west seems more of a charming discovery than a grand arrival. One is brought up almost to the elevation of the doorway by a short flight of steps from the sidewalk. A partially-covered pergola, with a trellis structure almost overcome with wisteria, leads past panels of industrial sash which illuminate the interior. The dim pergola soon terminates under the high freestanding portico. Directly ahead stand the doors to the original Sunday School (now known as the Fireplace room). Subtle devices – a step before the door, the lack of a dedicated gable or shed roof – scale back the importance of this entry in favour of its twin on the left.

Approaching the main entry from the south, along the gentle rise of the scored-concrete walk, the high portico creates a monumental space over the intersection of the axes. The exposed structure of the sheltering hood creates an outdoor vestibule where a brief pause comes naturally. The cornerstone tablet stands to one side, its cast-concrete lettering and lightly-pigmented frame catching the light from above. Originally, a small decorative fountain stood nearby. The main approach is compressed back to human scale by a low roof immediately over the entry doors. The overall progressive effect from street to door is quietly grand at first, then humbling, in preparation for the breathtaking revelation of the interior space.

An interior of carefully managed light, space and colour

Once inside, a small, low-ceilinged passage (later enclosed by a second set of doors) continues the feeling of compression begun by the gable roof over the door just outside. Moving towards the light of the narthex one begins to appreciate that the materials truly are the same inside as out. Sunlight is filtered through the blue–grey, hand-hammered panes of Belgian glass, sending broad sheets of light across the aisles at regular intervals. Skylights maintain the flow of sunlight to the narthex where the entry doors and Fireplace room intercept it on the Dwight Way side. Above the steel sash and concrete pillars, the low ceilings of the aisles are finished in rough-sawn sheathing, alternating 10 and 2in widths, nailed to 4 x 4in rafters. The wider boards are stained light grey, the narrower strips a darker blue-grey, setting up a polychrome rhythm echoed throughout the structure.[34]

To the right of the entry, and projecting back towards the street behind a sliding steel sash panel, is the original Sunday School, now aptly named the Fireplace room. It is a simple hall dominated by the monumental, vertically-oriented fireplace on the east wall. It would seem more like a dim, Gothic refectory but for the sunlight which floods in from the south-facing wall of glazed factory sash. The vernacular spirit of Maybeck's domestic architecture is clearly expressed here in the exposed roof

31 Southwest corner of the church today, sheltered by dense landscaping.
32 Main entry axis, flanked by trellis structures. Shadows from the high portico roof are cast in front of the entry doors.
33 Original Sunday School, now called the Fireplace room. Maybeck's Arts and Crafts period domestic design spirit predominates, from the massive chimney to the furnishings and lighting fixtures.

32

33

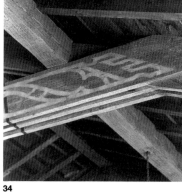

34

35

34 Fireplace room. Stencilled trusses are three boards which pierce the roof, then interlock with beams resting on south elevation columns.

35 First Reader's room. Maybeck designed chairs and tables for the Readers' rooms and board room situated behind the concrete screen and velvet panels at the front of the auditorium. Most of these pieces are now used in the Fireplace room.

36 Brightly decorated gable beams catch light from the south tracery window. At night, blue and red lights shine from the fixture (left) to illuminate beams and ceiling.

37 Looking south, afternoon light fills the west aisle of the auditorium.

36

37

structure and heavy presence of the chimney. Trusses, purlins and rafters are each stained a different hue, as if colour-coded according to purpose. A tracery design decorates the bottom chord of each truss, the centre of which is stained light grey to match the concrete of the chimney whose tapering shape at the same height is echoed by black outlines on the trusses. A home-like atmosphere is suggested by the simple Arts and Crafts redwood lighting fixtures – three-dimensional square crosses with metal caps and bare bulbs at the ends. In its current use as a meeting room, the table and chairs, all designed by Maybeck from English precedent, are gathered around the fireplace as naturally as if pulled up around the hearth at a friend's home.[35]

Across the narthex, on a diagonal opposite the Fireplace room, stands a bank of swinging oak doors which open to the spectacular main auditorium space. The simultaneous intimacy and majesty of this

vast hall is dreamlike, but the first impression – an overwhelming visual commotion of details – slowly gives way to reveal a coherent and highly-ordered decorative and structural system.

Maybeck's own words – 'the plan is the backbone of anything beautiful' – help to clarify an understanding of the interior and its complex and varied elements. The plan of the auditorium (as the main worship space is known in a Christian Science edifice) is a square or 'Greek' cross. Overhead, two clerestory levels form a volume of overlapping square crosses. The north end of these extends to accommodate the organ loft which rises to the highest roof level. To maximize the drama and practical use of the auditorium, Maybeck spanned the central space (40 ft²) with two pairs of crossed trusses, each a variation of the Pratt truss, patented by Thomas and Caleb Pratt in 1844. This was an unusual structural choice for a church interior, since Pratt trusses were used primarily for railroad bridges during the second half of the nineteenth century.[36] Here, a paired version of the trusses was designed to spring from each of four pentagonal piers which stand at the inside corners of the square cross plan. The piers carry the load of the massive trusses and are buttressed in turn by the clerestory walls which meet at a 90-degree angle at the backs of the piers.

Applied decoration as the exponent of structure

What appears to be decorative chaos in the auditorium in fact demonstrates a well-reasoned hierarchy. Christian Schneckenburger, the painting contractor hired to execute the delicate stencilling throughout the church, was a professional artist brought from New York to help prepare buildings for the expositions in San Francisco and San Diego of 1915. A sympathy clearly existed between Maybeck's design and Schneckenburger's execution of it. They understood each others talents and limitations. Maybeck praised Schneckenburger's work in the church, saying that he had 'made a wonderful job of it'.[37]

Overall, the decorative elements of the interior become richer and more expressive as they progress from floor to ceiling. At floor level, materials are left plain. The concrete piers, smooth at the bottom, become fluted only above the level of the pews. Painted decoration begins where the clerestory walls join the backs of the main piers. Triangular iron plates hold 10 x 10in Oregon pine posts in place, and a monochrome stencilled design overlaps both bracket and post to emphasize and celebrate the connection. Multi-coloured triangles at the tops of the piers' flutes form the transition to the elaborate cast-concrete capitals. The capitals themselves are nominally Romanesque in design, but include the Byzantine element of a rich palette of colour to brighten the woven basket shapes and swirling shafts of the miniature pilasters. The composition becomes even more complex above the capitals. Two layers of corbelled brackets and a layer of crossed blocks build up

38

39

to the spring-point for the trusses. In a characteristically romantic gesture, Maybeck reversed out his wife Annie's initials in the gold paint on each corbel.

At the clerestory height, the ceiling treatment becomes even more complex. The ceiling is dominated by gilt, profiled corbels which extend through the wall, past the ornate tracery windows to become rustic, unpainted exterior beams. Alternating 10 and 2in boards sheath the ceiling's background area as in the narthex and aisles, but groups of three 2 x 4in purlins, spaced three inches apart, take the place of the single 4 x 4in purlins on the lower ceilings. Progressing further up the decorative hierarchy, the major crossed trusses are boxed structural frames whose side and bottom lengths are filled with Gothic tracery panels, installed in continuous bands. Behind each panel, iron tension rods, the signature feature of the Pratt truss, are bolted to the bottom chords and fitted snugly into angled notches. This connection is emphasized by yet another stencilled design. The decorative tracery motif within each of the panels reflects the placement of the hidden tension rods: the reverse curve of the Gothic ogee describes the diagonal angle of the rods. Similarly, the vertical panels themselves correspond to the vertical compression posts of the truss. The multitude of gilded tracery panels catch the light from below, turning the otherwise dim truss and rafter area into a heaven of aurora-like reflections. Adding to this are more than 20 hanging 'pew lamps' suspended from the ceiling to a

height about 12ft above the floor. Intended to provide light for responsive readings, they also cast light through their trefoil cutouts to create a sea of delicate starlights. Above, the climactic intersection of the Pratt trusses – the point of greatest structural compression – is where Maybeck and Schneckenburger expended maximum decorative effort, expressing function as form at the literal and figurative high point of the auditorium.

The interior's north elevation is also dominated by Gothic tracery. A concrete screen, pierced with large quatrefoils, stands behind each of the two chairs on the dais behind the Reader's desk, located in the front of the auditorium where an altar would stand in a church of a different faith. Behind the screens, a panel of deep-burgundy velvet softens the hard predominance of concrete. The screens lend an aura of significance and consequence to the recitations of the two readers, but manage to do so without over-elevating

the status of the individuals themselves, as can often be the case in traditional pulpits. The base of the Reader's desk is also concrete, its coloured floral design deriving from a construction complication as the concrete was poured into board forms. These were lined with paper to ensure a smooth finished surface. The paper wrinkled in the process, however, causing indentations to run the height of the desk's base. Instead of ordering it to be filled or re-poured, Maybeck asked Schneckenburger to 'fix' it with paint. A charming decorative effect resulted in the most visible part of the church: the creases were artistically exploited to become tree trunks, with polychromatic branches painted directly on the concrete.[38]

38 Portion of main auditorium, looking south from the organ loft.

39 The main auditorium, looking east with the Reader's desk at left.

40 Interior detail of cast concrete capital with blocks and corbelled beams to support truss system. Note foul-air duct above capital, screened with a quatrefoil tracery panel.

41 Interior detail. Pratt trusses meeting above the centre of the auditorium. Colourful decorative stencilling symbolizes underlying hardware which stabilizes and fastens the junction. Tracery panels catch light cast by reflecting bowls below.

42 Buttressing side truss meets main truss, each containing Gothic ogee panels whose diagonal reflects the position of the iron tension rod behind it. Note black notches that secure the iron rods.

40

41

42

43

44

43 Centre aisle, looking south from the Reader's desk. An early plan for semi-circular seating was deleted in favour of one that allowed unobstructed views of everyone in the auditorium.

44 Sunday School addition designed in 1928 by Henry Gutterson in collaboration with Maybeck. A straightforward hall, the interior uses a decorative and structural vocabulary similar to the main church.

45 Interior, looking north, c1913. Note hanging metal stars at organ loft level. These were installed by church members but later removed reportedly because they created a distraction during services.

Above the Reader's desk a balcony rail, pierced with Gothic quatrefoils, conceals the organ console, behind which a gilt tracery screen supported by gold columns stands in front of the pipes. Late in life, Maybeck said he was unhappy with the screen in front of the pipes and even denied designing it.[39] It appears in the earliest archive photographs and blueprints, however, along with pressed-tin ornaments which were suspended like stars amid the tracery screen. Church members had hand-sewn the ornaments, attaching them to wires according to Maybeck's design, but they were ultimately removed reportedly because they distracted members during the services.

A legacy of timeless beauty

Even if it were to be stripped of its prodigious decoration, Maybeck's auditorium would still define a noteworthy and dramatic space. But without the gilt tracery panels to give depth and life to the trusses, or the decorative stencilling to announce the structural functions, the space, if left undecorated, would have been merely rustic, or even gloomy. Instead, where materials meet, polychrome patterns celebrate the connection. Where structure is hidden, the opportunity is exploited to mark the place with a colourful statement. Strategic touches of blue, red, green and gold animate the wood, concrete and metal surfaces, vividly bringing to life Maybeck's playful sense of colour.

Maybeck had written that he favoured H H Richardson's Trinity Church, Boston (1873–7) above other churches.[40] He undoubtedly studied its square plan and lavish use of decorative colour on the interior, but it is a facile solution to suggest that Trinity, or any other structure, was the inspiration for First Church of Christ, Scientist. Trinity can be considered as one of the many antecedents which made an

impression on Maybeck's work, but ultimately, First Church of Christ, Scientist is so fresh and wholly new that to belabour historical comparisons is to miss the point. Maybeck was creating straight from the heart. Inspired by the sincerity and creative instincts of the church membership, he designed as he did because he believed that those who had sought him represented a deep-seated faith which was beginning to reassert itself after a millennium's silence. The resulting edifice transcends period styles and spans the centuries as surely as Maybeck put himself, as he said, 'into the shoes of a twelfth-century man'.[41] Through the medium of concrete, steel sash and wood, First Church of Christ, Scientist is ultimately the legacy which most thoroughly expresses Maybeck's firmly-held belief in the ideal of beauty.

The Sunday School

In 1928, when Maybeck was 66, the church membership asked him to design a Sunday School structure to be contiguous with the main church on the east side. Henry Gutterson, a talented Berkeley architect and member of the church, was appointed architect in charge with Maybeck available to oversee. Maybeck claimed to have drawn the elevations.[42] The pastels which survive are unsigned, but they do bear the characteristic expressiveness and detailing of Maybeck's earlier drawings for the church.

45

The Sunday School wing extends east along Dwight Way, beginning with office space which backs up to the Fireplace room, then turns a right angle to the north at the Sunday School entry from the street. An exterior trellis structure nearly identical to the original for the main church continues along the sidewalk in front of the Sunday School addition, using the original molds to cast the distinctive capitals. The school's entry doors are carried out in a Gothic tracery design carved in wood and glazed with diamond-leaded art glass. Overhead stands a freestanding portico, a smaller version of the entry treatment for the main church. Inside, the philosophy of exposed structure and exuberant decoration is faithfully carried out. Many details are reminiscent of the main auditorium, which undoubtedly prepares young students for a comfortably familiar transition to the main building. The composite whole suffers, however, without the benefit of the arrestingly unusual volume and plan of the main church.

Despite his close involvement in the Sunday School, Maybeck complained that the lot was too narrow to do a proper job of the addition. The remark may have been calculated to distance himself from the final result, much as he had disowned the organ screen in the main auditorium when shown a picture of it in the 1950s. But whatever Maybeck's view, the addition is a sympathetically-designed space. It ultimately cannot compete, however, with its neighbouring source of inspiration, just as nearly any other structure would suffer in the same comparison – simply by reason of proximity.

The future of Maybeck's masterpiece
The membership of First Church of Christ, Scientist, Berkeley have continuously demonstrated their appreciation for the significance of the architecture they helped to create. Their respect for the building as a design achievement is as strong as their affection for the creative spirit of Bernard Ralph Maybeck. Maintenance and conservation of the building is assigned to a full-time professional and alterations, when undertaken at all, follow careful design criteria and are sensitively executed to honour the spirit of the original work. The firmest guarantee of the building's future as a church, however, is that its members understand now, as they did in 1910, how their edifice demonstrates the essential link between the material world and the metaphysical underpinnings of Christian Science. As a result, Bernard Maybeck's vision of faith as form perseveres as the greatest tribute to his art.

46

46 A venerable wisteria fulfills the original landscape plan as it wraps around massive trellis posts to root the structure literally and figuratively to its site.
47 East elevation from garden court. Pairs of exposed beam ends under the eaves are joined with filler blocks – carved members that do not extend to the interior but merely enhance the visual support of the projecting roof.
48 Main entry to Sunday School annex, with freestanding portico similar to main church entry.

47

48

Notes

24

1 Kenneth H Cardwell, *Bernard Maybeck: artisan, architect, artist.* Santa Barbara and Salt Lake City: Peregrine Smith, Inc., 1977, pp.13–16.

2 Bernard Maybeck, taped interview conducted by Robert Schultz in February 1953 for the radio station KPFA in Berkeley, California. Documents Collection, College of Environmental Design, University of California, Berkeley; hereafter cited as KPFA interview.

3 Cardwell op. cit. p.16.

4 Cardwell op. cit. p.17. Sara Boutelle, in her work on Julia Morgan, states that the Ecole des Beaux-Arts accepted only the top 30 applicants when Morgan tried for admission in 1897 and, successfully, in 1898. See Sara Holmes Boutelle, *Julia Morgan, Architect.* New York: Abbeville Press, 1988, p.30.

5 KPFA interview.

6 Sally B Woodbridge, *Bernard Maybeck: visionary architect.* New York, London, Paris: Abbeville Press, 1992, p.19.

7 ibid, p.20.

8 Richard Longstreth, *On the Edge of the World: four architects in San Francisco at the turn of the century.* New York: The Architectural History Foundation and Cambridge, Mass. and London: MIT Press, 1983, p.389 n. 28.

9 Leslie Mandelson Freudenheim and Elisabeth Sussman, *Building with Nature: roots of the San Francisco Bay region tradition.* Santa Barbara and Salt Lake City: Peregrine Smith, Inc., 1974, p.5.

10 Robert W Winter (ed.) *Arts and Crafts Architects in California.* Washington DC: Preservation Press, 1994 (forthcoming). See discussion of the Swedenborgian Church in the chapter entitled 'A C Schweinfurth'. See also Freudenheim op. cit. for an investigation of Worcester's influence.

11 Charles Keeler, *The Simple Home,* with a new introduction by Dimitri Shipounoff. Reprint of the first edition published by Paul Elder, San Francisco, 1904. Santa Barbara and Salt Lake City: Peregrine Smith, Inc., 1979, p.xxiii.

12 Keeler, Charles, *Friends Bearing Torches,* an unpublished manuscript of personal reminiscences begun in 1934, Keeler Papers, Bancroft Library, University of California, Berkeley, p.223.

13 Charles Keeler, *The Simple Home* op. cit. p.5.

14 Mary Baker Eddy, *Manual of The Mother Church: The First Church of Christ, Scientist in Boston, Massachusetts,* 89th edition, published by the Trustees under the Will of Mary Baker G Eddy, Boston, copyright 1895 and 1936, p.60.

15 Archives of First Church of Christ, Scientist, Berkeley, hereafter cited as Church archives. Minutes of the Board of Directors, 31 March 1905.

16 Church archives, minutes of the Board of Directors, 1 June 1905.

17 Church archives, minutes of the Plans Committee, a sub-committee of the Building Committee. In addition to Eulora M Jennings, a noted local artist, the Plans Committee included Helen P Smyth, Josephine S Snook, Elizabeth Watson (secretary) and Eleanor Juster.

18 Sara Holmes Boutelle, *Julia Morgan, Architect.* New York: Abbeville Press, 1988, p.30.

19 Church archives, notes kept by Eulora Jennings, chair of the Plans Committee.

20 Bernard Maybeck, from 'An interview with Mr Ralph Bernard (sic) Maybeck, architect of the edifice of First Church of Christ, Scientist of Berkeley, December 1953'. Typescript of a taped interview conducted by church members Don and Clara Owen. Church archives.

21 Rebecca Howell, 'Rebecca Howell interview'. Typescript of an interview recorded by church members Nadine Graham, Don Owen and Clara Owen on 1 March 1964. Church archives.

22 Church archives, Building Committee minutes, 27 March 1911 and Ruth Gordon, 'Partners in the book trade: Paul Elder and Morgan Shepard', *Quarterly News-Letter,* 43, spring 1982, p.36. I am grateful to Albert Sperisen and Ann Whipple of the Book Club of California for providing the latter.

23 Church archives. Undated, unsigned document which describes the needs and desires of the church membership with regard to their new church edifice. Hereafter cited as design programme. The handwriting appears to be the same as in other documents signed by Eulora Jennings.

24 Church archives, 'Report of the Plans Committee', dated 17 January 1910, signed by five members of the committee. The report defends the action taken to hire an architect, reminding the Building Committee of the motion passed by them: 'that the Committee on Plans be authorized to employ an architect or take such action as may seem wise to secure plans ... We regret that any misunderstanding should have arisen in the minds of the Building Committee ... It is of vastly more importance that we fit together as stone upon stone than that we have a material structure'.

25 KPFA interview. Maybeck's remarks on how he categorized his clients include: 'My customers are classified. I've tried to find out ... how I'm going to classify them historically ... starting with Gothic, [etc.]'.

26 Typescript of a taped interview with Maybeck, op cit.

27 Church archives, design programme.

28 The entry gate was executed but never installed. It is now in the collection of the Oakland Museum.

29 Church archives, minutes of the Building Committee.

30 Church archives, minutes of the Board of Directors.

31 Rebecca Howell interview.

32 Church archives, design programme. Maybeck was credited for inspiring some of the writing in the programme, possibly including this passage: '[the church] should express *sincerity* and *honesty* as exemplified in the use of genuine construction and materials which are what they claim to be and are not imitations in treatment or method of use of something else'.

33 Carbon copy of a letter dated 23 March 1910 from Maybeck & White, Architects, to Detroit Steel Products Company, Detroit, Michigan. Documents Collection, College of Environmental Design, University of California, Berkeley.

34 Church archives, contractor's specifications.

35 Church archives, Furnishings Committee notes and Building Committee minutes. These notes confirm that Maybeck designed the tables and chairs. Also, correspondence between A J Forbes & Son and C F Wieland (Documents Collection, College of Environmental Design, University of California, Berkeley) confirm that the furniture was manufactured by A J Forbes & Son, successor firm to Alexander Forbes who made the chairs for the San Francisco Swedenborgian Church in 1894. The Maybeck chairs closely resemble chairs made by English Arts and Crafts figure Ernest Gimson, after a design by Philip Clisett. Maybeck may have been aware of the Gimson chairs as they were widely exhibited in London and elsewhere during his travels for the University of California competition. See Mary Greensted, *The Arts and Crafts Movement in the Cotswolds.* Stroud, Glos. and Dover, New Hampshire: Alan Sutton Publishing Ltd, 1993, pp.13, 159, and ill. *94.*

36 Carl W Condit, *American Building.* Chicago and London: The University of Chicago Press, 1968, pp.96–7.

37 Owen interview; contains several of Maybeck's references to the quality of Schnekenburger's work.

38 Christian Schneckenburger's role in the painting of the Reader's desk base is recounted by Maybeck in the Owen interview. Maybeck related the story: 'I had to make [the Reader's desk] out of concrete, of course, and so as to make it smooth I put some tar paper on the inside and when I poured the concrete into it it made wrinkles, and then these wrinkles showed ... I told [Schnekenburger], "Now about those cracks that are there. Could you fix it?" So he used the cracks for branches and put leaves all over the branches. It made the loveliest possible kind of a picture'. Maybeck scholar Kenneth Cardwell questions this story, however, suggesting that the wrinkling was planned, or at least expected, and that Maybeck had conspired with Schnekenburger to create the effect.

39 In the Owen interview, Maybeck asserts that the screen in front of the organ pipes had been added. Maybeck's memory may have been failing, however, since the screen shows up on the original drawings and in the earliest extant interior photograph, taken before the interior appointments had been completed.

40 Woodbridge op. cit. p.91.

41 cf. note 25.

42 According to his own statements in the Owen interview, Maybeck drew the elevations, but Gutterson performed the balance of the design work for the 1928 Sunday School addition.

Previous page Main chimney, west elevation (the flue extension is not original). Coloured cathedral glass fills the industrial sash at organ-loft level.

Left Northwest corner at side entrance, showing the dynamics of the overhanging eaves at both clerestory levels.

Centre South elevation, showing freestanding cast-concrete columns surmounted by trellis structures. Profiled beam ends extend from interior truss chords in the Fireplace room.

Right The high main portico on the south elevation stands adjacent to a cast-concrete and wood pergola structure, which carries the wisteria vine as originally proposed.

28 **Left** East elevation from the garden court. Pairs of exposed beam ends under the eaves are joined with filler blocks – carved members that do not extend to the interior but merely enhance the visual support of the projecting roof.
Right Heavy structural elaboration is elevated to a design statement in Maybeck's scheme for the trellis and entry portico on the south elevation.

30 **Left** A pergola-covered walk from the southwest corner shelters the secondary entry axis. A giant sequoia, part of the original plan, dominates the structure.
Centre An ornate copper downspout to the right of the main entry doors reflects the architect's concern for comprehensive design control.
Right Main entry to the church, looking north from Dwight Way. The high portico, lush plantings and lack of stairs provide a welcoming and easy entry for everyone.

32   Main auditorium, looking north.
Massive concrete piers support
wooden blocks and corbels,
which spring to the main truss
system. Hammered-metal pew
lamps and reflector bowls with
trefoil cutouts cast light in all
directions, picking out details in
the gilded Gothic tracery panels
overhead. The pervasive historically derived forms are enlivened
and made entirely new by the
exuberant use of colourful
decoration.

Left The windowless upper clerestory level is dominated by gilded Gothic tracery panels set into the truss system.

Centre, above Colour-coded ceiling sheathing, purlins and rafters form a decorative structural backdrop for the main trusses and hanging light fixtures.

Centre, below A triangular iron bracket secures a timber post to its concrete pier base. Stencilled painting decoratively merges materials.

Right, above Gilded inside and unpainted outside, a series of paired beams – carved and separated by blocks – extend through the south tracery window to support the eaves.

Right, below Fireplace room. Stencilled triple truss chords pierce the roof to interlock with beams resting on the south elevation's trellis columns.

Left Nominally Romanesque, the cast-concrete capitals of the main interior piers also include Byzantine-inspired decorative accents of rich colour.

Right The capitals terminate in two layers of corbelled brackets and a layer of crossed blocks, built up to the spring-point for the trusses.

38 **Left, above** At the north end
(front) of the auditorium, a gilt
tracery screen springs from gold
columns between the organ
console and the pipes.

Left, below The south tracery
window acts as a fanlight to
flood the back of the auditorium
with afternoon light.

Right Main auditorium, looking
towards the southeast corner.
The space forms a square,
bi-axially symmetrical cross.

Left Creases in the paper-lined board forms caused unintended wrinkles in the concrete base of the Reader's desk. These were decorated to resemble tree trunks, with polychrome branches painted directly on the concrete.

Right On the dais behind the concrete Reader's desk, screens pierced with large quatrefoils rise to decorated spheres and blocks which in turn build up to support the organ-loft balcony.

42 **Left** Built-in music cabinet, a Maybeck design, is positioned between industrial sashes at the west end of the narthex.
Right West aisle, looking south. Post and beam structural composition allows natural light to flood auditorium through large expanses of steel sash filled with antique art glass.

Left Fireplace room, formerly the Sunday School. A home-like atmosphere is suggested by the simple Arts and Crafts redwood lighting fixtures, and by the table and chairs designed by Maybeck. The monumental chimney strongly recalls the architect's typical domestic designs.

Right First Reader's room. Below the organ loft at the north end of the structure, the small office is panelled in simple board and batten, and furnished with Maybeck's designs.

Left Entry, south elevation of the Sunday School addition, 1928. Similar to the main church, a portico rises over the approach to the entry doors and Gothic tracery appears in windows behind the narthex. Columns are cast from the original 1910 trellis column moulds.

Centre Interior detail of the Sunday School addition. Main piers terminate in tracery-panelled capitals, which hint of boxed Pratt trusses in the main auditorium.

Right Sunday School auditorium. The details and decorative exuberance are reminiscent of the main church, visually preparing young students for the transition to the adults' auditorium.

48   Architect's presentation renderings of (above) south elevation,
showing vine-covered pergola
and trellis structures much as
they still appear each spring, and
(below) west elevation
looking north, showing the
deep overhang of eaves.

The following drawings are based on Maybeck's own working drawings; some details were modified during construction.

Location map

1 First Church of
Christ, Scientist,
Berkeley
2 University of
California at Berkeley

Berkeley

Shattuck Avenue

Bancroft Way

Dwight Way

Bowditch Street

Telegraph Avenue

College Avenue

Ashby

Ashby Avenue

2

0   1km

0   3000ft

Site plan

1 First Church of
Christ, Scientist,
Berkeley
2 Vedanta Society,
Berkeley
3 University of
California halls of
residence
4 American Baptist
Seminary of the
West
5 University of
California building
6 Private apartment
building
7 People's Park

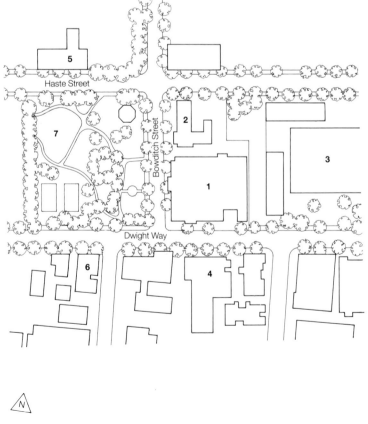

5

Haste Street

2

7

Bowditch Street

1

3

Dwight Way

6

4

0   50m

0   150ft

Floor plans

1 portico
2 pergola
3 entrance
4 narthex (lobby)
5 Sunday School
  (now called Fireplace room)
6 dressing room
7 main auditorium
8 aisle
9 Reader's desk

10 rear hallway
11 Usher's room
12 Board of Directors' room
13 First Reader's room
14 Second Reader's room
15 rear entrance
16 Janitor's room
17 office
18 side entrance
19 organ gallery

50

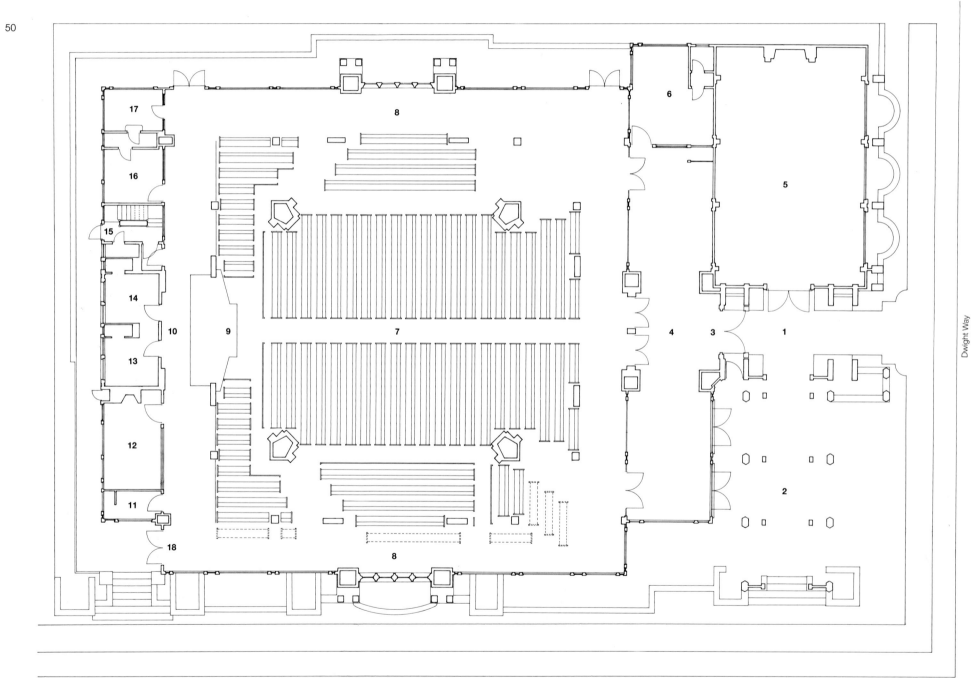

Ground floor

Bowditch Street

Dwight Way